INCANTATIONS FOR REST

Poems, Meditations, and Other Magic

ATENA O. DANNER

SKINNER HOUSE BOOKS

BOSTON

skinnerhouse.org

Printed in the United States

Cover art: "Untitled" by Naimah Thomas
Cover design by Tim Holtz
Text design by Jeff Miller
Author photo by Rebecca Harris

print ISBN: 978-1-55896-888-2
eBook ISBN: 978-1-55896-889-9

5 4 3 2
26 25 24 23

Cataloging-in-Publication data on file with the Library of Congress

"The Divine Audacity of Bree Newsome" was previously published
in *understory quarterly*, no. 1: winter 2021.

"Reckon: Reclaim" was previously published in Transformative
Spaces, May 28, 2021. transformativespaces.org/2021/05/28/
poems-for-people-who-arent-ready-to-move-on

CONTENTS

PREFACE

Like most poets, I write poems out of the wild need of my own chaotic id. And by catching strains of ancestral voices that cling to my spirit. And by capturing those brief, blessed moments of understanding the song of the earth. Many of the poems here began that way. Given the opportunity to share my work with a wider audience via the inSpirit series, I felt a responsibility to cultivate my writing with more intention. As an unapologetically Black writer, I wondered how I might serve my people. As a Unitarian Universalist, I considered what I might offer the wider faith community. So I set out to offer something needful.

At the very least, I hoped to create some healing and joy for myself as a Black UU by writing some of the poems that I would have wanted to read during my experiences with Unitarian Universalism over the years: the joys and sorrows of this faith life. My deepest hope is that I could relate the depth of my love for my people and the extent to which I have hope for beloved community. To remind folks that they are connected. To add my candle to the vigil for human imagination. To craft a soft, dark place for someone to rest.

I recommitted myself to writing every day and added structure to my reflections. I sought out communities of writers and gratefully drank in their wisdom. Reconnecting with art outside of my own talent kept me connected with the joy and beauty of other kinds of creativity and kept me from becoming obtuse or obsessed. This was my work: to become a vessel for whatever might be possible, doing my best to trust that I was worthy enough. This collection is the result of my developing discipline and persistent faith.

Here you will find poems, reflections, litanies, and other types of verse to reflect on privately or in community. I hope there is some resonance here for anyone seeking it.

Poetry has healed me and held me and saved me so many times. In my effort to offer that to someone else, I have been fortunate enough to connect more deeply with myself and my purpose as a writer: to create connection; to honor my ancestors; to celebrate my culture, and to invite myself to practice rest, healing, grief, and love. These are all gifts, and I am so grateful.

ACKNOWLEDGMENTS

First, love and respect to my mother, Marilynn, who is the daughter of Dorothy, who was the daughter of Ada: she is the first Black woman I saw writing routinely, seriously.

Honor and gratitude to my ancestors. Your labor and suffering will be accounted for. Honor to my father, Aten, who is the son of Lorraine, who was the daughter of Ossie: he gave me the gift of always knowing that I am an artist.

To my children: Thanks for your patience, your light, and your shadows. And your love.

To Chris: for everything. Every day.

Love, love, love to my siblings from Team Sankofa for helping me realize my worth and for loving me with the most abundant generosity. Ashé!

I am grateful through the marrow of my bones for the support of Sher, Emily, Anita, Kelly, and Tanuja for talking and reading and encouraging me along this path.

I am blessed beyond measure to have had the support of communities of writers whose thoughtful prompts, kind encouragement, and rigorous, critical feedback have helped shape so much of the work in this collection. Thank you, Split This Rock. Thank you, Surviving the Mic. Thank you, Hurston/Wright Writer's Week folks. Thank you to the communities of Care + Create and the Hibernation Den. I could not have done this alone. I am grateful.

STORYTELLER'S INVOCATION

Honor our Ancestors
Stories tucked into our hearts

Bless the stories reaching back
To when the Word began

Blessings to my siblings
As we break the Word apart

Touch the soul inside of it
And build the Word again.

DECATUR, GEORGIA CREEKS

Coolness. The quenching splash of shadow at the tree
    line
I had never been hot in Michigan—not really.

The cool promise of moving water, rushing over clay
    and concrete:
That "Shhhhhhhh . . ." that "Whhhhhhhhh . . . !" that
    "Tep. Tep. Tep. Tep . . ."
At the park so my brothers can play ball, honor their
    rituals
I am six, here because my brothers have to watch me.
My new friend Neenee is here because she wants to be.
Neenee is seven—a wild girl. Cusses, loud. Doesn't wear
    shoes.
Doesn't ask permission. Neenee just does. I cannot
    comprehend.
Possessed of herself, she approaches the creek, announces
    a crawfish sighting;
draws me irresistibly to the water's edge.
My older brothers aren't watching, so I don't ask
A tender thrill of near disobedience in my gut.
I touch the water; this is how it begins.

Next summer: soaked and sandy, we walk along the
    creek bed.
Between each careful step we hear
that "Shhhhhhhh . . ." hear that

"Whhhhhhhhh . . . !" hear that little splash,
little plop, little splash . . .
Paradise of flow and motion
Every step a problem to solve:
Stability of surface + texture equals rock or log?
Depth of water versus width of walkable bank;
visibility versus chances of snakes
equals paths and ways and days and days . . .

Small, brown, and dusty, we walked all over to safely
　　enter our paradise,
in the street, along the tree line,
across a stranger's yard (borrow their hose for a drink)
I think back on it now, wonder How?!
So small! Where were our mothers?!
A short time after the Atlanta child murders
we splashed gleeful miles below common sightlines,
in the company of who-knows-how-many ghosts . . .

Once boys threw rocks at us as we walked home.
Followed us along, striking closer, harder
Not on our block—a ways from home,
teeth and knuckles closing in.
Desperate, I ran up a stranger's steps
opened the door bold, stepped in like I knew them.
That lady was ready to put us right back out,
but kindly allowed a phone call once I explained.
I spoke urgently to my mother; Neenee stood back
smashing silent tears off of hot cheeks.

Later, escorted by two of my five brothers, we returned
　　to the ambush site
that very same day.

I have wondered my entire adulthood
about the mechanism of that liberty . . .
Was I watched more closely than I thought?
more trusted than I expected?
Or was it (as it often is for us) simple necessity?
Tightrope-walking Black mamas over a threadbare
　　safety net;
the need to be elsewhere
to hope for the best and lean on prayer?
Whatever it was, here's the outcome:

I have strategies for crossing over water;
for following my gut and finding my way home.

When I fret about my kids and "will they be safe?"
My childhood is what I remember.
Not because they are safe, or because I was safe,
but because I remember what it felt like to feel like
I was free.
And to know my parents didn't give that to me.

How will these children learn to listen, to trust
their senses, their
instincts, their
own heartbeats
with mine pulsing loudly in their ears?
There's no way but away from my side. Simple necessity.

I succumb to this choice with my heart in my throat,
testing that vein of faith:
Trust that they can find their way over,
trust them to make their way home.

MENDING

If you are feeling worn thin
and riddled with holes,
I hope you will take comfort
in the fact that much can be mended.

Mending comes in many forms,
and be aware: mending won't make a thing new.
You will be the same as what makes you you.
Yourself patched up:
pulled together and swiftly sewn.
If you've got time for darning,
it is work, work, work:
tedious as meditation
and sometimes as rewarding—
just do what you have time for.

My fabric has a lot of holes;
I'm grateful for
the stars I can see through them, the sunlight warming
    my blood.
I mend some, I leave some
mend some, leave some,
patching in remnants of steel wire and
my own voice: "You deserve."
"It will be okay."
"Keep going keep going keep going
keep sewing."
Truth holds together, and I wear the truth I've told.

When places in life tear and wear thin,
examine the frayed edges and threadbare patches.
And if they tear, appreciate the light coming in
as you learn how best to mend.

PRAYER FOR ARTISTS AND CREATIVES

Blessed be the persistent; may we honor our routines.
Blessed be the audacious; may we take risks.
Blessed be the humble; may we learn to fail and to learn
     from failure.
Blessed be the curious; may we play and discover.
Blessed be community; may we turn toward each other.

ANCESTORS OF THE PAGE AND THE CALL

Elders of the Message
not quiet, not easy, not waiting another moment
Ntozake, Toni, Octavia, Pauli,
Zora, June, Gwendolyn, my mother (not an ancestor,
    but a lit fuse . . .)

To my Ancestors and Elders: I honor you all!
My mother spoke to me in your language, so I would
    be ready for this religion.
I take up the mantle
and bear the reverberations—the power! It shakes me!
    I plant my feet . . .

Ntozake did not come for your comfort: none of y'all.
Mother Morrison did not come to suffer fools.
Octavia E. has an omen for you
Did you think Reverend Dr. Murray would let you off
    the hook?
Zora gave less of what the world wanted
and more of what we needed: what needed to be said.
June said it plain and simply undeniable.
Gwendolyn's quiet pace dogs your steps and keeps
    coming and coming and coming . . .

The moment I touch the page, I'm howling the through-
    line, tasting
the blood and joy.

CONSPIRACY

What if we tried
to breathe together?
Pull in, pull deep,
release together?

What would be born
from a unified fulfilment
of the bodily self
and its undeniable need?

What if we all try to breathe together?

A shared breath is a moment:
Refreshment and
a reminder of our more-than-oneness.
And if we continue, if we
slow and quicken apace with each other,
a murmuration of lungs becomes
one organ, singing.
And if we continue—learn each other's rhythms
over time,
rising and falling like waves,
we become a perfect thing:
A conspiracy dancing
a dance of need and met need,
request and offering:
Feeding each other.

What if we decided to breathe together?

What if we open the airways?
What if we unblock
unbind
unfetter
the hands that feed us?
The Earth, the air and the water that hold us and
    shape us
were breathing together before we found ourselves
    existing.
And so they will continue
after we're gone.
Imagine our final goodbye coming later than sooner;
imagine our final breaths in paradise. . . .

It's not too late to slow down, fall into the dance,
catch the vibrating air and release our lungs into song.
Anything breathing cannot help but breathe,
but breathing together is a choice we make.

SHARING

I scraped my bits of clay together
until I had a hand to reach out with,
then shared what I had.

I sang myself together
until my voice could be heard again,
then offered a song of comfort.

My friends and I pour the same water
 between our cups, taking turns.
Everyone thirsty; no one dried out.
This is how we survive the drought.

OF THE ALTAR

We always had altars growing up,
spread with books and art,
carved totems, and other artifacts of Blackness:
Always a copy of *Jambalaya*.
We were conspicuously   areligious
but Spirit hung and drifted through our home   like oily
incense smoke.
Cowries, papyrus, woven kente: we laid such longing
on fabric
Calling out to Africa;   belief in an unheard echo.

Our ways were lived if not explained,   so when I had
my own home,
a nesting bird,   I gathered bits of life
in the shape of a hand:

Bits of poetry, dried roses,   fabric I wove at school,
burning candles   and Egyptian musk,
silver ankh on a leather cord . . .
Using language I didn't know   was language
Learning how to say *need*   and *home*.
To speak, casting prayers and gratitudes,
A sacred space to connect   and return.
To joyfully sing our ancestors home,
Keep ritual,   remember and learn.
Now I come before the altar as never before,
to tend to my heart   and call on my magic.

SINGING PRAYER

I give thanks for this time
I give thanks for this space
I give thanks for us all who have come to this place
That we breathe the same air
For the work that we share
I give thanks, I give thanks, I give thanks!

EVOLUTION OF WORSHIP

First there was metal and fire
Then water, beings, and bodies
Something some way in the ether
had the knowing to draw them together

First Sun and Sky by my father
then Church by my great-grandmother
I gathered from things seen and unsaid
that neither was more than the other

First there was flesh and water
and then there was flesh and water
And then there was flesh and water again—
our story, our path: our nature

In my hands I hold metal and fire
I look to sun and sky
I live in the flesh and the water
Receiving, I tend to my altar

LINEAGE OF MAGIC

Where does your magic come from?
Can you recount the lineage of your power?

How we wield the wisdom
of our elders and ancestors matters.
To know that their spells are our spells . . .
To recognize when we speak their incantations . . .
We must learn to own, for better or worse
that their power is our power.

If I name the generations
and acknowledge every predecessor,
could my faith survive knowing
the name of my teacher's teacher's teacher?
Can I face all the ways my
knowledge (which is power) traveled from hand to hand
    to hand?

Be suspicious of power
cut off from its source.
Knowing is power, and naming is power.
How can you measure what you cannot acknowledge?
How can we wisely wield what we cannot perceive?
What can be solved which is not believed?
How will you learn the history of your magic?

Learn the names and
speak the names and
know the lessons
and teach the names.
Earning is a part of learning; it keeps us from stealing
and from clumsily, harmfully wielding.

FACEBOOK VESPERS

Timestamp: 7:16 PM

[*Image text (black words on a background of slender, white silhouettes of trees) reads:* What fortifies your spirit?]

Apart from time, we gather in this age of isolation,
We catch as catch can for restoration
Evensong building across the wires:

May I be cared for and not lonely
May I know peace, alone or together
May I know beauty, and may beauty exist unseen
I give thanks for Nature: earth and water and fire;
I give thanks for the Word: story and poem and song.
May I share my gifts of creation, as I am comforted by
    the gifts of others.
May I be inspired by courageous struggle, and may
    others be inspired by me.

We manage to—need to—be together
As we find the song, we sing.
May it be so.
All at once or as you need.

SIMPLE PARTS OF FAITH

I believe in my breath and heartbeat,
in the woven, grasping roots of trees.
I may not see or hear how things move underneath,
still, I believe.

I believe in my slow return to the Earth
in the simple quintessence of darkness.
The necessity of light and heat,
in my oneness with water, I believe.

Every swallow a prayer,
every waking an answer,
each moment we reach toward safety: an invocation
The simplest acts of faith.

Because I believe in the power of words,
of intention expressed, of gratitude and creation,
the unfurling of purposeful language
might be a prayer or incantation

Every time I seek out more
than what is already there,
A prayer, a prayer!

SHARING LOSSES

Loss binds us together
undeniably.
Like the aching low moan
of a cello—you feel it first;
other senses follow—
feel it in that place
where the keening cry of a wounded heart begins.
In loss we could be family.
In that shared knowing and need;
in these chances to rebirth kindness to each other.

SWIMMING ALONE

My pulse still quickens
as I step into the cold, sharp tide,
step toward something remembered . . .
The smell of the water does its conjuring work:
regret flashes across my thoughts: tiny silver fish
lingering a moment, then quickly gone.
A memory drifts before me, ghost of light
Here and gone but still obscuring my vision.

The drop-off is sudden and steep—
I know it's there; never know exactly where.
I might still fall forward and sink into that depth:
dark and seemingly still,
but for one, irresistible, current.
Mostly, though, I've learned to stay a few steps—
a few swaying breaths—from the edge.

THE DIVINE AUDACITY OF BREE NEWSOME

When I saw Bree Newsome on that line
Spirit laid a hand on me:
"Be still, be still . . . Watch and listen
how the world becomes bigger;
expands on the inhale,
right before the shout."

I watched a Black woman rise
I watched a monument fall limp
by her anointed hand—
the sheer, audacious simplicity of it!
Her Declaration of freedom, decision, dominion.

While I watched Bree Newsome's divine work
 I forgot that I was flesh
and burned white-hot
Sparks spilling out of the sides of my mouth
Her Message changing me, charging me:
"I did it because I am free."

RECKON: RECLAIM

When you say you know
the relationship "isn't perfect"
and it's code for all the red flags
dotting your lawn, telling you where
not to dig . . .

How long have we been grieving the truth?

When you fear the end of your
weekend even as it begins,
and in the last hours pretend not to know
that you do not know how you'll survive
going back,
reaching into yourself
to give your warm will over again . . .

How long have we been grieving our freedom?

When you reconnect with an old friend
who reminds you of what could have been,
who knows who you used to be and could be again,
so your whole self pulls toward that feeling
like a magnet
dizzy with the force of worth . . .

How long have we been grieving our safety?

The slithering haze of capitalism is thick and invisible
Pushing into your lungs, you can taste

its saccharine notes in the back of your throat
every time you breathe . . .
How long have we been choking and heaving?
So busy coughing we forgot that we're still breathing
We forget: we are still here.

It's time to admit that we've known
it's been so bad for so long: lifetimes
before these fourteen, fifteen, eighteen months . . .

How long have we been bereft and mourning?
Grieving our star-filled skies, our gardens, our homes?
Our sleep, our laughter, our people?

Our right to create sanctuary
is as fundamental as our heartbeats and dreaming
As necessary as skin touching skin.

This season of reap and reckon,
with enough hot screams and tears
to fill the cold sky with clouds,
has also ushered in the clearing of air
that necessarily follows the storm:
A taste of clean rain
A glimpse of blue sky
A whiff of rich earth
A touch of warm comfort
after days and days and days . . .

Remember what we were told to learn to live without.
Remember all we were told we should throw away?

Bless the dirt-streaked rebellion of tending our gardens;
may we always choose to feed ourselves and each other.
Power to the sleepers, faithfully napping
Healing and restoring: Rest is wealth
that we must reclaim and redistribute.
Look to the wise:
disabled, divergent, and distant,
who mapped the smooth, blank spaces
Who find water in places
that many write off as wasteland.

They covered our medicine with trash:
Let's take it back!
Let's choose a world we can heal in
Choose air and water and earth, again and again;
choose laughter and care and warm skin.
If we learn to protect our collectiveness
it can carry the weight of our grief like nothing else can.
Let's be wolves who walked back through the veil
electrified, hungry, and ready to fight.

CHANGELING GENERATION

Who knows how to bring up a changeling generation?
Wave upon wave, they come.
Our fear of magic is not theirs to answer for.
We had one job. We have one job.

Trick babies, changing faces, changing places
all along the way.
How will we know the chrysalis from the rest of their
    iridescent selfhood?
To recognize their true forms, we must unclutch rusty
    fingers
and let go, let go, let go.
Let them turn and try on all the jewels
Turn and see their shifting colors
Watch as they hold themselves up to the light
Turn, turn, turn—surprised by the beauty
By boundless possibility . . . !

We have one job.
To bring up a changeling child, you must pour love into
    an active volcano
Tossing food and care into the searing mouth
Sometimes falling in. And crawling out.
Falling and crawling again and again and again,
keeping faith in rich soil for future gardens.
You will not survive it on your own.
And we cannot survive without them.

The world has stolen nothing, has given us the children
    we need.
Earth more generous than we may deserve.
Protect these babies: furnace-forged
trickster children with sparks in their smiles,
chewing metal where we suckled stone.
What we called death, they call transformation
Where we saw fearful endings, they invite us, laughing,
    to begin.

TEACHER TO TEACHER TO TEACHER

For J. Cox

When you took the time to recognize
what I was doing well,
you were measuring water into the mouth
of a desert-parched little girl.

Now I carry a pitcher,
treasured legacy in my hand. I offer
witness: a voice to say, "I see you."
affirm, "What you can do matters."
argue, "You have something good to share."

Thank you for those flowers planted,
for my sacred mandate to scatter seeds
into every crack in the concrete;
into every unclenched, opening hand.

DIVINE RIGHT TO REST

My blood is full of farming; farming that didn't feed us.
My blood is full of church, and I dream about trains to
    cities.
I wake up before I'm ready; before I'm ready I go to work.

Church to escape the fields? Trains to make it to Sunday?

Work is a slow burn; sleep is fat
The kind your brain is made of.
Eat and feed: the system is a cycle. Not a seesaw.

"We have come to serve man. Soylent Black is . . . ?"

Have you ever sat in a hospital chapel without sighing?
Go ahead and sigh. Have you ever dozed off
in church? It's the perfect place. Go ahead.

Would your divine creator begrudge you a little break?

Stillness is our primal becoming: how we
live up to ourselves. Makes the most; shapes action.
A beating heart rests every chance it gets.

LITANY FOR THE EXHAUSTED

I don't want to do things. Don't want to get out of bed.
Don't want to get in the shower. Don't want to care what
time it is.

I don't want to answer to "How are you doing?" I don't
want to answer to "How are the kids?" Don't want to
scan for something to say. I don't want to answer.

I don't want to cajole or convince or coerce. I don't want
to be responsible. Don't want to be the adult. Not ready
to move on; don't want to forgive.

I don't want to smile. I don't want to code switch, don't
want to do co-worker small talk. I do not want to meet.
Don't want to get back on track. Don't want to clear up
the confusion. Don't want to take the lead.

I don't want to dig any deeper and scrape the bottom.
I don't want to think about what that would mean . . .

I don't want to decide, to do or abide. I don't want to.
I don't want to.

LITANY OF OOPS AND OUCH

I receive your "Ouch" with openness and curiosity.

I receive your "Oops" with acceptance and empathy.

I offer my "Ouch" with hope and trust.

I offer my "Oops" with humility and courage.

I release my "Ouch" with immeasurable faith.

I release my "Oops" with purpose.

I release your "Ouch" with promise.

I release your "Oops" with my eyes and heart open.

LITANIES OF WORTHINESS

For affirmation:

I am worthy; I can be still; I will believe; I do belong
I am enough; I can receive; I will claim what I need;
    I deserve wholeness
I am important; I can take up space; I will not move;
    I matter
I am aware; I can listen; I will learn; I trust my wisdom

For humility:

I am open; I can discover; I will invite experience;
    I take risks
I am afraid; I can admit it; I will do what is right;
    I show up
I am tired; I can rest; I will slow down; I renew myself
I am full; I can share; I will offer what I have; I keep
    growing

Blessed be the vigilant—may they know rest.
Blessed be the vulnerable—may we learn from their
    courage.

LABYRINTH CHANT

Down the straight path
On the ground
On the leaves
Turning back
On the gravel
Wide around
Over leaves
Between the grass.
Overhead
Rustling sound
Leaves aloft
Falling down
As above
So below
Turning, turning as we go.
Past the garden
Bedded down
On the leaves
Across the path
By the ivy
Red and brown
On the hard clay
Curving 'round
On the gravel
Down the line.
Atop the clay

And pebbled stone
Make a way
Earth and blades
Turn again
Track apart
Final turn into the heart.

From the heart, first we turn:
Follow, turn,
And track apart.
Blades and earth
Way is made
By pebbled stone
Atop the clay
Down the lines
Gravel crunch
'round the curve
Cold, dense earth.
Brown and red
Ivy climbs
Across the path
Colors play
Put to bed,
The garden lies
Turning as we go along.
As below
So above
Some leaves fallen
Some aloft

Hear them rustle
Overhead
Grassy strip
Green and soft.
Coming 'round
Gravel trail
Sharply turning, turning 'round
On the leaf-strewn, sacred ground
Take the path
Straight line down.

BENEDICTION TO BUILD A WORLD

In what world are you powerful?
In this world we can build people power, together.

In what world do you act on knowledge and truth?
In this world we can learn and move toward justice together.

In what world do you hold to your values in the face of
    what scares you?
In this world we can affirm each other's resolve to do right together.

In what world are you confident in your worth?
In this world we can affirm that each of us is enough.

In what world do faith and beliefs guide your choices?
Together, we can build this world.

In what world can you learn from those with less power?
Together, we can build this world.

In what world could empathy shield you from judging
    others?
Together, we can build this world.

In what world will your power plant roots, and tend to
    branches and leaves?
Together, we can build that world.

PSALM OF TALENTS

It is medicine; I use it for healing
Like water: I fill my cup and pour into others
It is a gift: I cultivate inspiration
It is thread: I weave a map of connection
My power: I wield it for protection

A SPELL FOR WARRIORS AND HEROES

I say "No." With strength, with conviction,
Without blinking. I say "No."
   My yes is a gift to bestow and to receive.

I declare myself protected by organizing for collaboration,
   by delegating, by sharing.
I will work with people I can trust to hold what I put down.
By the power of asking for and receiving help,
I release control and call in opportunity.
   I make room to rest, imagine, and connect more deeply to my
   purpose.

I protect my relationships. I pour into them from my cup
of time. I start with myself. I lay down my important
work and seek rest.
   I gently cast aside compliments that elevate exhaustion
and sacrifice of wellness, and turn toward relationships.
I speak my intention for wellness into being, and into the
knowing of others. I claim time for relationships: for fam-
ily, friends, neighbors, pets . . . I show up for my own life.
   There is enough of me to be there for my people because I protect
   my time like I protect my people.

I accept my imperfection as natural: my own unmapped
   territory, my language to learn.
I map my own self
live in my own self
speak my own self

I create sanctuary with the resulting lessons—a land loving me gives me.

I let things go. I let go sooner than later.
I don't need wiggle room, I need a dance floor with a
   resting bench.
As I move to the dance floor, I open up space for another
   to succeed in the work
where I cannot/will not/don't want to.
I am one of many: intentionally decentered, blessedly
   replaceable;
forgiving, forgiven, and grateful for the lesson.
Others can bloom as I lay fallow.

I slow down
I call on discernment to examine the costs of speed,
   to ask
who gets left behind when I surge ahead?
I give myself over to my deepest senses to locate stories
   and histories beyond my own
and feel for the connections between us.
I cast away white supremacy culture: you will not
   prosper here!
You will burn away when confronted by wisdom and
   commitment
I call on the wisdom and commitment of my people,
   known and unknown
The wisdom our communities hold, in all its facets,
   reflections, and shadows,

will banish the illusions of efficiency being best for
    everyone
Of the clock being the same as time
Of the inconvenience of accountability and justice.
We cast out quiet exclusion of our siblings
    Together we grow toward liberation at the speed of care.

Ego, opportunity hoarding, perfectionism: *I cast you out!*
Low expectations, control, uncreative thinking: *I cast
    you out!*
Racism, ableism, sexism: *I cast you out!*

I call in the protective powers of respect, curiosity,
    vulnerability, grace, trust, care, and love:
cover me against the siren call of urgency and
    emergency.
I call on the powers of rest, play, and joy to stand
    between me and despair and burnout
I call on beloved community:
Guide me toward life, toward love, toward care.
May it be so, and blessed be!

THINKING OF MATHEW

For my beloved friend and comrade, Mathew P. Taylor

If you don't feel gratitude tonight, here—have some of
mine. My cup is full and overflowing. I have received
such a blessing. Take some and pass it along.

If you are feeling cold with loneliness tonight, come
close and share warmth against the chill. There is
enough of this radiant love.

Feeling unworthy? This table holds a cornucopia of
invitation, a feast of acceptance. And a place for you. Eat
and be full.

> Dear friend, your smile and your spirit have
> assured me. There is plenty. There is enough.
> We deserve it and it is ours.

RECIPROCITY

I put aloe on my skin and I
remembered . . .
Like a dream, I remembered being small,
fascinated as my father engraved a wooden sculpture.
I stood close because we were close; my father's creativity
was like my mother's immunity:
it carried and supplemented my own.
Standing stalk to my climbing vine,
by his side I could share the sunlight

Suddenly a bright flare of pain,
hissing steam, shocked my small frame rigid—

My father's fast and steady hands grabbed the aloe
from the windowsill.
Assuring, calm,
he broke it open and pressed the cool liquid to my
    burning skin.
This was my introduction to magic:
medicine in my own home!
An unforgettable lesson: the power of cultivation
to yield reciprocity.
We took care of the aloe vera, and the aloe took care
    of me.

Years later, I pull aloe from a yellow pot,
slender and bright green leaves, but brown and pinched
    at the base

choked by the wrong mix of soil
I nurse an ember of shame for not catching it sooner
In apology I place a leaf
in the arms of my altar goddess
Another accidentally cracks open: green clarity shines
as the gel flows into my hand.
I know at my core not to waste it.

My glistening hand finds a patch of eczema
The itch that has plagued me all morning is soothed.
My ember flares as I realize the extent of what I've done.
I can get a new plant, but I still regret this neglect.
I apologize to the aloe roots; resolve to give better care.
Even without roots, their precious gifts still care for me.
I place the final leaf on the altar, among the ancestors
to remind me:
How care extends and then returns;
our purpose to nurture each other.

SPIRIT DOES

Spirit announces itself:
faith overrides logic;
resonant song, radiant light.
Spirit turns us up and binds us together;
connections strengthened; awareness deepened.
Encompassing darkness, bone-deep vibration
Proprioceptive certainty
Humility: course-correction.
Follow these toward purpose
Slow down and feel
one sense at a time

ELECTION NIGHT 2020

For the BLUU Beloveds

Dear 2016 Self,

It's me, from 2020.
Before you ask, let me just tell you:
>   I am as terrified as you were.
>   I wish I could say that this part has changed.

I have no idea what is going to happen tonight.
I did make sure of one thing, though:
>   we won't be alone this time around.
>   We got us: we'll face what's coming holding each
>   other.

EVERY STORM RUNS OUT OF RAIN

The storm don't steer the ship.
Storm may push it, toss it, rock it, roll it, crack it,
even sink it.
But it takes a knowing mind and guiding sense to steer a
    ship toward safety.
It takes a memory of the harbor haven
to guide a body soaked with fear, pushing
against the wind

It takes faith to hold out
for the storm to run out of rain.

BLESSING OF THE INSTIGATORS

with honor and gratitude to Surviving the Mic

Bless the table shakers,
the talkers-out-of-turn,
the power confounders and mic-takers,
agenda breakers.
Bless the bridge burners:
protecting the village by any means necessary.

Peace be to the bummer-outers,
the conversation dead-stoppers,
naked emperor shouters,
eggshell stompers:
as you receive whispers and private notes of agreement,
may solidarity illuminate your courageous path.

These are the movements that knock us loose
Shake us into the sky and out toward the stars
These are the impacts that force us together
Drive our roots downward, to reach for each other

GIVING EACH OTHER OUR FLOWERS

For Black women, femmes, and genderqueer people everywhere

The sun was near to setting
and just steps from our party of three
at the North Shore suburban Ravinia Festival
a wide circle was drawn on the crowded lawn:
twenty chairs and a long table draped in silver.
It was clear from their outfits and the space they took up
rites of celebration were being observed. And then, she
    appeared . . . !

Tall! Shoulders back, and just so . . . comfortable. She
    came to let us know,
"I see you ladies!"
Priestess of the Sisterhood of Tight Jeans, periwinkle
    braids piled up, blending with the twilight,
undercut, beneficent smile,
she initiated the Ritual Exchange of Compliments,
    which naturally we returned.
A volley of blossoming flowers, escalating like fireworks!
    The easy delight of confessing admiration!
She was glad to take a picture of us—
"I'll come back and take a pic with y'all later!"
And she floated back to her circle of sisters on a cloud
    of joy.

Black women/my siblings/my sisters are a marvel.
How many times have these moments turned my day
    around?
The gentle touch of a sister's words, saying,
"Hey girl, I see you! Love that outfit!"
"Okay, red shoes!"
"Go 'head with those braids!"
"Come THROUGH, goddess! Yes!"
"I see you!" I *love* us. Seeing each other in joy and beauty
is an act of resistance: defiance!
Surveilled one moment, invisible the next, they tell us:
"We are watching you and no, you don't matter."
Our rituals, scattered and spontaneous
are life-giving. Lifesaving.
"I see you." I got you. I love us. We got us.

HUMBLE YOURSELF BEFORE THE BRUTAL LESSONS OF THE FREE BLACK CHILD!

My children are of another world; have glimpsed their
    Godhood already,
but haven't grasped mortality. My clumsy, dangerous
    babies.
I'm attempting complex spellwork in the dark: no muscle
    memory, no teacher.
What little I know is cellular, what little I remember:
    ancestral.

I hold my Godlings underwater; they thrash until they
    realize
they are breathing
and need not destroy me.
One day their Godhood will outgrow mine,
and they will swim beyond my reach, as it should be.

If I am a wolf, you are a lion
If I am a river, you are a rock
If I am a star, you are a nova:
Did I birth a black hole and/or galaxy?

If you're an explosion, I'll be a controlled burn
If you're a sharp edge, I'm a tempered blade.
If we fight and I lose,
It was so you could learn to lose and survive—
Listen! To lose—
Pay attention! And to learn
to survive.

COMBING LITURGY

Melt under warm, oiled fingers parting hair, drawing
lines. Nothing says "you're safe" like a rat-tail drawing a
firm line across a giving scalp. Hand of God guides head
to knee to rest. Shoulders fly up to shield from lightning-
strike hands solving knots, flinch against the pull, pull
away from heat rolling in like thunder: not a forgiving
God. Piano-grade percussion: fingers hit the jar, work
the comb, and play the anthem again and again up and
down the crown-to-be. Again and again until the work
gets done. This is the devotional language: song learned
by singing, dance learned by moving, prayers learned by
crying and healing . . . praying from the bottom up;
medicine rubbed into the skin.

A NORMAL CONVERSATION ABOUT
ATTENDING UU CHURCHES

Look—damage has been *done*.
Sometimes I slip through unhealed cuts
and for a while, slip away.

> Seventeen years, and one person asked me, "Aren't
> you tired?"
> When I'm tired is when I stop *coming*. Then, they don't
> see me.
> Because if I don't see myself, why keep looking
> at a mirror that doesn't reflect?

That time those white people heard their white UU
    minister tell his congregation
they need not fear Black Lives Matter activists because
    they "do not threaten violence in the same way as
    Malcolm X . . ."
(I know. I KNOW.)
. . . did anyone comprehend how terribly wrong that
    went?
If we pass out and die from sheer exhaustion at coffee
    hour
will anyone realize that the entropic slide into violence
was theirs to embrace or avoid?

> They don't even notice we left, until they need some
> representation—

Mmm-hmm—

and find that they have come up short.

They be looking for brown faces the way you look for
loose change.

They'll be like, "wasn't there   ?" "Didn't we have   ?"
"I can't quite remember her name, but she was here
for some time. . . ." Knowing full well you never even
asked my name.

They'll say something like, "Our community isn't for the
faint of heart!

[chuckle, chuckle, self-congratulatory chuckle!]"

Seriously, though—it's not funny to be exacerbating
heart issues.

Cortisol levels in Black UUs on Sunday morning
ain't no joke.

Should we speak again and again
when the air around us holds stubbornly still?
Should I keep talking until I suffocate?
I did not come here to be a ghost.

If we all supposed to be in the same faith, and they
wanna worship together,

They **need** to learn curiosity.

Y'all better learn how to learn!

Let curiosity lead them past

"Where are the brown faces, that we might count
them?"

(May I remind you: that question *has* been answered);

I mean . . . Worry about their *own* selves, as in:
*Why would we even **want** to be among you?*
What sanctuary is even available
to shelter from the pain that whiteness
  was created
to create?
They don't even *know*.

UNCONDITIONAL EARTH

Earth hears our crying and answers, exasperated:
"Balance will come, one way or another."

Still, Earth abides its children, healing, already reaching
    out to take
what we don't know how to release. Forgiving the
    clumsiness, searching for hurt,
to seize the worm of our collectively poisoned hearts
and resolutely cast it out;
we shout and jerk away, snapping it off.
The gnawing head of suffering remains intact
and Earth must start all over again;
human behavior all over again.
We are always afraid, but a little braver each time . . .

Earth resigned with expectation:
To love and outlive another child.

IN DARKNESS, ALL THINGS ARE POSSIBLE

Realize that we were taught
to fear the dark.

Consider the seed that splits and unfurls
unseen within the Earth . . .
Consider the inside of the egg;
consider the place where
the Big Bang exploded . . .

Unknown and generative,
darkness is unpredictable:
limitless possibility.
We are in the habit
of learning to fear our potential,
but imagine embracing rest and dreams . . .

We learned early to believe in
the whiteness of certain magic and light
And blackness of certain arts and hearts;
confronted with the sky and its stars, I must reject this
    entire premise.

Remind me, siblings
to unlearn these bad habits
and accept the gifts I've been given.
Darkness is free and abundant;

There is joy in unfurling
from the shadows we were made in.
We need only close our eyes to go home.

MYOB

It is a lovely late morning. The day is brightening after stops and starts of rainfall, and I'm staying outside for a while so Sissy Dog can dry off in the sun. It's lovely to listen to drops of water falling from the trees as the sunshine warms and cools; a slow pulsing of daylight. The breeze feels cool and friendly on my skin. I've been watching the bees flying along the ground. They thread low through the grass at a slow, bobbing tease. I assume they are looking for water. I want to help them look for it. In my mind, I am willing them toward the shady places of the yard that are abundant with droplets, gathered on blades of grass and tops of forgotten cans. As I silently urge their gentle dancing, I imagine my hands waving them gently toward water. I feel the tension of it in my hands as I fill with want: to solve this problem for them, to guide them toward the answer. And then this occurs to me: any self-propelled being that lives knows how to find water. If this is the problem, it is not mine to presume to solve. The birds, the squirrels, the bees, Sissy Dog, and me have been doing just fine here in the back yard: coexisting and minding our own business.

A BLACK DAUGHTER SPEAKS OF RIVERS

My blood swims in every
   water way,   every tributary
   between here and the Delta
  Layers of my lineage are pounded into
 hot red clay, tint the rings of trees,
  are hewn across the scarred fields of southern farms.
 From the striving metal of plows and   guns,
shifting whorls of fingerprint echo across state lines on
 train car railings and travelling shoes,
 sacks and cases clutched in hands,
   rare and luminous keys and pens;
 I know our blood runs over and under the dirt;
   that our ghosts get louder as you
   follow down the Illinois
      Central Line, and along its
      connections . . .
       from Mississippi and Tennessee
        tracking north
        and leaning
       on the sun

My family is not a tree, but a river
Four streams in before our story gets lost
in the din of the Mighty Mississippi,
on to ancestor oceans, impossibly vast.

My great, great, great-grandmothers are likely
Mollie
Missouri
Malvina
Adaline . . .
Features   inked out
by the   Blackness of their living
Details erased
by the whiteness of record
I know you are written somewhere: name
and story:
planters' ledger
colonizer's census
family bible
newspaper
or grave . . .
I need to *know*
and speak your names.

GENERATIONAL WEALTH

My grandmother was so tired
that my mother was born tired.
My Mama's so tired
that I'm tired right now. And I see
my children getting tired,
so it's time to put this to bed.

I will gift time to my children;
they will inherit a legacy of resting:

Leisure time and vacation days taken,
sick time used to nap and renew.
I'll steal time and show them how to eat it raw,
I'll say "Yes!" to my babies, on the clock,
show them how to tuck joy and stillness
into the pockets of reclaimed life.

When I accrue time: I let them see how I use it.
When I take time: I give it to them and let them play.
I save time in their names, for them to practice how to
    protect it
and spend it on rest.

It has been said that the best things in life are free;
    untrue!
The high cost of the best things in life is time!
My progeny will know that time seeds restoration:
how creativity is nurtured by time to play,

how love is deepened by time together,
how revolution needs time to imagine,
how healing and growing are possible and what it takes
to rebuild broken skin and bone.
That wellness is rest is time is wealth.

PRAISE SONG FOR A DESERT ROCK

How can so much grow out of a rock? It is a dry, hot,
   living thing.
Earth beneath my feet: unfamiliar, so I take care—a
   visitor here.
I was invited into the desert by my friend, a guest herself.
I arrived, was greeted by the heat and the rock. Bare and
   black earth, decorated
with sharp greens and tiny flashes of flower
I offered respect to the land, animals, ambassador trees

A hum, low and droning in the arid air—an
   acknowledgement; a question.
I promised to return, went off to make my greetings.

Where I live, the native rock is buried or carried away.
Here, this consciousness was nearer to the surface and
   easier to hear ,
how it called to me and expected an answer.
Mornings later I would slip away: some prayers and some
   first-time encounters are private. This Rock! A force,
   calling out to my spirit; I realized a gift was due.
The animals eyed me—the lone male, a pig named
   Steve, grunted his noisy warnings.
I bowed my thanks as a guest: treading lightly among
   the trees, not knowing the customs:
"My respect, my humble gratitude . . ."
The rock hummed, then spoke

"Sing to me, won't you?" What could I say but
"Yes, of course."
A tone deep as cactus roots welled up to fill my throat,
    spilled out
Poured from my mouth, shimmering above the rock face
then blended with the tremulous, grey-streaked hum of
    the earth.

I don't really comprehend the age and size of the world,
but I know I am a part of it. A single life among billions
is as big as any star.

SPITTING OUT ROCKS

For the first time, I confessed to a group of colleagues,
     white women,
that I don't believe in "assuming good intentions."
Imagine the reaction to such blasphemy.
While their eyes pressed against me, bright and buzzing
     with nerves
I closed my own just briefly, felt some weight lift away,
rolled my shoulders into a new lightness.
There is a heavy cost to swallowing the truth.
I've been tumbling rocks in my mouth for decades;
smooth yet jagged, they cut my tongue.
Stinging relents with each stone that drops from my
     cotton mouth.

Across the twin arcs of my shoulder blades, I feel a
     prickling: sensation returning
 at my core: a presence awakening
Flex and release
Reaching . . . release: stronger
Extending with every truth I risk,
turning slowly outward with every breath.
Stretch and—
arch back electric as the tips of bones break through!

A slicing sound as reaching arms unfold out of my back
and feathers, slowly turning, shine like blades in the
     light.

INSTINCTS

Dear Manic Beaver,
You were in so much pain, trying to build a dam
through the deluge. You're still angry
at the storm for what was lost, at the wind
for what you couldn't hold. I'm sorry
you didn't know how to stop working. I'm sorry so much
was washed away.

Dear Lonely Bird,
Your song was lovely and your dance was
entrancing; the pebbles you offered—so bright!
You did what you were supposed to do, and still
for all your fluttering and gathering . . . Well, I am sorry
for your disappointment,
that your shiny things were accepted then pushed aside.

Dear Wounded Fox,
Your howling is perfect: clear, loud,
and heartbreaking. I'm so sorry
you had to free yourself after days and nights of hunger
and weakening blood.

Dear Wild Animal,
You deserve a warm, safe place. And you will have one.
Keep building, keep giving
Keep hunting. But first,

Rest.

ATTENTION DEFICIT INVOCATIONS

I prayed myself awake because sleep was groundless
    falling:
no perspective, no visible horizon.
I prayed for noise because danger was quiet; I was
    wary of stillness and ease.
I prayed for deliverance from things forgotten,
    "Dear God,
I pray I don't hurt anyone;
I pray the damage can be undone.
Dear God, let me prove myself worthy . . . !" For this
    I prayed, again and again.

My faith was in my failure.
A home without sanctuary aches:
wearing down the body that cannot rest,
and straining the ever-bracing heart.

To those waiting on your own self-betrayal, my hope
    for you is trust,
rooted deep in love and unfolding, reaching out green
    for the sun.
To the vigilant and worn, counting on failure, my
    hope for you is rest,
and the cooling balm of forgiveness:
Forgive yourself; it wasn't your fault.
Forgive yourself; it wasn't your fault.

Forgive yourself; it wasn't your fault.
Forgive yourself; it wasn't your fault.

May we all know the drift of peaceful sleep;
may we all know the ease of safe home.

DEAR FEAR,

I see you, Fear. I hear you. I know you.
I'm not mad at you and I don't believe you.
Fear, you are like my teenage child. Sibling. Self.
You flinch and you protect. You warn. You need rest.
Let me relieve you, guard you while you sleep.
I see you still and breathing.
I gently close the door
and step away.

EARTHEN VESSEL

I wind down to a slow tick of breath
that allows some room for humming
I can see all the women in me dancing a cartographic
    dance,
mapping this life with their thousands of steps and stops
When the music washes over them, I am delighted:
How many of them sing along!

I am the hands
 I am the vessel
I am the water, the earth, the well
I am the clay, the jar: filled with grain,
with seed, with root,
with life, decay, and dust.

Magma, shift: I am that flowing
I am the body, strata stacked
Touch the ground and you'll feel the heart of the world
calling its whole self home.

REVENGE BEDTIME CONTEMPLATION

That moment when the last kid settles down
is like the sun rising:
The warmth of aloneness spreads across silence,
as cautious as a parent's measured, retreating breaths.

Exhilarating as flying in a dream: fast and high,
through epic vistas of moonlit clouds and stars—
practically giddy! Defiantly sacred:
this stolen space for self within stillness,
delicious and intoxicating.

Time melts and pours, runs over my tongue
I breathe deep
and sigh . . .
Spending time like I've got plenty of it.

Racking up debt, the bill will come due,
but that's hours away
Hours away . . .

STORIES AND STARS

For Del (and Lifted Voices)

Each of us is a shining rock
Sparkling dirt and metal
crackling with power

Each of us is flung around the Universe
Time-travelling in machines
of anxiety and optimism

Each of us is a speck of dust
Each of us is God
We are the stars we gaze upon

Every star in a constellation
burns up gas on its own, and yet all
are connected in story, collectively known

We are siblings in story.
We'll be together again: in orbit
or in the telling.

KUUMBA AND THE FOURTH PRINCIPLE

This essay was presented to the community of Black Lives of Unitarian Universalist Beloveds during our 2020 Kwanzaa online celebration. The original presentation included media and liturgical elements that are unavailable in this format and has been modified for coherence in the absence of those features.

With deep love and gratitude to my beloved Team Sankofa siblings.

The Sixth Principle of Kwanzaa is Kuumba, or Creativity. We are going to reflect on the principle of creativity as it relates to BLUU's Fourth Principle, "Experimentation and innovation must be built into our work."

Reflecting on these Principles together, let's consider our duty to embrace the best tools, practices, and tactics in our journey toward liberation. This absolutely, uncompromisingly requires creativity and imagination.

Our history, our truths, our resilience: Creativity helps us hold on to our stories and lineage. Our art tells the story of our existence, our survival, and our self-determination. Creativity harnesses the imagination—imaginings of what is not yet, but *could* be—and if we feed it, it builds the world out of pasts, present, and futures. And how do we feed it? Creativity feeds creativity, which means art begets art and inspiration multiplies itself.

To this point, I want to share a story with you about ancestors Nina Simone and Lorraine Hansberry. Lorraine Hansberry was recorded speaking a powerful phrase of truth and affirmation to a group of young writers: that they were "young, gifted, and Black." Hansberry had already marked the significance of these words as the title of one of her plays. Nina Simone's creative contribution has turned that phrase into a call to manifest brilliance in our young people that reverberates across the decades.

How many lives continue to be impacted by Nina Simone's elaboration on that phrase? Do you see it? How our creatives shape our lives by telling our truths and making space for us in futures where others do not see us? Imagination is prophecy in the right hands. Creativity can turn into destiny.

Now, a personal story: In October of 2015, I participated in disrupting an international gathering of police chiefs with a force of creative organizers, blocking access outside and inside a conference center in Chicago. I had never seen such an elaborate, imaginatively planned protest. I saw things that I never considered possible until that day. Afterward, I was invited to be a founding member of Lifted Voices, a collective of Black and Brown women and femmes organizing for self-defense and liberatory action.

Fast-forward a couple of months. That December our collective organized an anti-incarceration memorial blockade, using hundreds of white origami flowers to represent the number of people lost to police violence in Chicago. The first memorial, which had been held one year prior, featured the handmade flowers. The year this second picture was taken, we took those same flowers, affixed them to LED lights, and used them to decorate the blockade lock boxes in the spirit of the holidays. Above the folks lying on the ground, blocking the street, I was walking up and down the intersection belting Christmas carols into a megaphone.

The creative presentation was not only intriguing to onlookers (both in person and on social media, which we used for raising bail funds), it was exciting to the people putting their bodies on the line to take action against mass incarceration and state violence. When you know you're probably going to jail, every bit of uplift matters. The people on the ground with their arms locked together were all arrested. After they were bailed out, the money left over from fundraising their bail was used to bail out a pregnant Chicago mom who had been in Cook County Jail for months for acting in self-defense and ending her abusive partner's life. That young woman was then able to spend Christmas—and eventually give birth to her baby—at home instead of behind bars.

I have been a part of many such actions, singing and reading poetry to the crowds. Pop-up galleries are created from signs and installations at these events, theater is produced in the streets, and people stand out in the cold and sit on the hard ground for long hours with songs on their lips and in their hearts.

Without creativity, the experimentation and innovation that BLUU's Fourth Principle calls for are inaccessible to us. Without imagination, our movements will stagnate, and we will recycle the same problems and ineffective solutions over and over again. Our lives are predicted, manifested, and recorded by the power of creativity. And each of us is imbued with some measure of the power to imagine and create, which Octavia E. Butler would have told you is less about inspiration and more about creating habits.

So the final reflection I will invite you into is this: Octavia E. Butler had a habit of affirmation, where she laid claim to her future by naming the successes she would have. She did this for years, and she made good on it by cultivating a discipline—a habit—of creative writing. Her affirmations were repeatedly marked by the same phrase: "So be it. See to it."

So, in the spirit of Kuumba, I ask: what will we be? What will we see to together? What kind of beloved community will we create, and how will we innovate and experiment our way into liberation?

Blessed be. Amen. Ashé.